In Praise of the Irish

Photographs from The Source Collection, Dublin
Edited by Michael Downey
With an Introduction by Andrew M. Greeley

Continuum   New York

1985
The Continuum Publishing Company
370 Lexington Avenue, New York, N.Y. 10017

Printed in the United States of America

Library of Congress Catalog Card Number: 84-72951
ISBN: 0-8264-0354-9

In Praise of the Irish

Introduction

We were sitting in Enis in the County Clare in the summer of 1976 at an Irish summer institute celebrating in theory the Irish contribution to American life. Like most meetings of Irish intellectuals, the conference was both an orgy of self-hatred and an orgy of the drink being taken.

My two colleagues (a sociologist and his poetic wife) had stirred up the animosity of some of the locals because we were celebrating our Irish heritage and they wanted to disengage from it.

Finally, long after closing, one of the women Irish intellectuals stared balefully into her dark guiness and grudgingly summed the discussion. "Sure," she said, "You Yanks will be Irish long after we're indistinguishable from the floating Belgians!" (She didn't say "floating" of course.)

In the context of the conversation she was right. After five hundred years of foreign occupation, much of the Irish elite is victimized by the self-hatred that is a mirror image of the contempt of the occupying power. In recent years they've been lamenting that hard times will erode what little cultural distinction remains in their land. A few years ago prosperity was supposed to do the same thing.

In fact, the vision of an Ireland indistinguishable from Belgium is so passionately beloved by your Irish elites that it has replaced the Creed as their statement of faith.

They are of course wrong about everyone save themselves. In fact, they are even wrong about themselves although they don't realize it.

The Irish are incorrigibly Irish, no matter how hard their English critics and their own self-hating intelligensia try to persuade them to stop being Irish. We went through the same thing in this country, doing our best to stop being Irish as the presumed price of being accepted as successful Americans. Well, we became successful, we're not accepted, and we're still Irish.

If your Irish sociologists want to know what an Irishman is like when he is educated, affluent, and successful, they ought not to look at Belgium, they ought to look at the American Irish.

This charming volume with its wonderful pictures explains why the Irish can't change even if they/we try. They/we are different, that's why. Much of what shaped Europe, for weal and woe, didn't happen in Ireland, or to the extent that it did, the impact was filtered through England. Ireland has deeper and stronger and cleaner roots in its own antiquity than any other nation in Europe. The late Poet Laureate, God forgive him for it, called the Irish the last Stone Age people. While that was calumny, it is surely true that in Ireland links between antiquity and modernity are much more intimate.

Curiously and characteristically, some of the Irish elites are trying to give that up just when the rest of the world is discovering that it's valuable.

With the poverty depicted in these pictures we can do without, but with the character and the vision and the faith and nature mysticism (brilliantly realized today in the poems of Seamus Heaney) we can celebrate.

Hence this book tells us why the Irish will always be Irish and why the rest of the world is fortunate that is so. Give yourself over to the celebration of Ireland.

ANDREW M. GREELEY

Mysterious Island

The Irish have captured the world's imagination, and the game of interpreting them has been going in for centuries, often with doubtful results.

Anonymous

My house stands on a lake, but it stands also on the sea. Waterlilies meet the golden seaweed. It is as if in the faery land of Connemara at the extreme end of Europe, the incongruous flowed together at last; and the sweet and bitter blended.

Oliver St. John Gogarty.

You feel the material world is rendered unreal and rather childish because it is overshadowed by the spiritual...shopkeepers do not seem to be real shopkeepers but to be pretending to be shopkeepers.

H. V. Morton.

And still the thoughts of Ireland brood
Upon her holy quietude

James Clarence Mangan

Tread softly because you tread on my dreams.

W. B. Yeats

It Could Have Been Worse ...

It seems impossible to distill the essence of the Irish spirit, to analyze its blend of practical and poetic, humorous and fantastic, sentimental and cynical.

Richard Kain: *Dublin*

May your soul be in heaven half an hour before the devil knows you're dead!

Irish proverb

When something happens to you in Germany, when you miss a train, break a leg, go bankrupt, we say: It couldn't have been any worse; whatever happens is always the worst. With the Irish, it is almost the opposite: If you break a leg, miss a train, go bankrupt, they say: it could have been worse; instead of a leg, you might have broken your neck, instead of a train, you might have missed heaven, and instead of going bankrupt, you might have lost your peace of mind and going bankrupt is no reason at all for that.

Heinrich Böll: *An Irish Diary*

They (the Irish) think that the greatest pleasure is not to work, and the greatest wealth is to enjoy liberty.

Giraldus, a Welshman, in the 12th century.

The Men That God Made Mad . . .

When Irish eyes are smiling
All the world is bright and gay.

Popular song

I am of Ireland,
And of the holy land
  Of Ireland.
Good Sir, pray I thee,
For of *saint charité*
Come and dance with me
  In Ireland.

Anonymous (14th cent.)

In Ireland the inevitable never happens, the unexpected always.

Mahaffy

For the great Gaels of Ireland
Are the men that God made mad,
For all their wars are merry,
And all their songs are sad.

G. K. Chesterton

An Island of Dreamers

The lights jig in the river
With a concertina movement
and the sun comes up in the morning
Like barley-sugar on the water
And the mist on the Wicklow hills
Is close.

Louis McNeice: *Dublin*

Even today Ireland seems to visitors a land whose enchantment is impossible to resist. The ever-changing skies bathe city and country in a magical aura. The intermittent sunshine, diffused by masses of cloud, touches grey rock and green meadow with vivid patches of light and shade. Colour effects are constantly changing in an uncluttered landscape.

Richard Kain: *Dublin*

Erin, the tear and the smile in thine eyes
Blend like the rainbow that hangs in the skies:
Shining through sorrow' stream,
Sad'ning through pleasure's beam,
Thy suns with doubtful gleam,
Weep while they rise.

Thomas Moore

Perverse and Irrational?

It was altogether a very jolly life that I led in Ireland . . . The Irish people did not murder me, nor did they even break my head. I soon found them to be good-humoured, clever — the working classes much more intelligent than those of England — economical and hospitable . . . But they are perverse, irrational, and but little bound by the love of truth.

Anthony Trollope

You don't have to be a peace-seeker to be happy in Ireland, but if you are you will find what you seek.

from *Conor Cruise O'Brien Introduces Ireland*

Three accomplishments well regarded in Ireland: a clever verse, music on the harp, the art of shaving faces.

Three things that foster high spirits: self-esteem, drunkenness, courting.

Three things that are always ready in a decent man's house: beer, a bath, a good fire.

Thomas Kinsella: *The Triads of Ireland* (tr)

Splendour of Fire

I arise today
Through the strength of heaven:
Light of sun,
Radiance of moon,
Splendour of fire,
Speed of lightning,
Swiftness of wind,
Depth of sea,
Stability of earth,
Firmness of rock.

from St. Patrick's Breastplate, 8th century.

It is a fatal mistake to begin by under-estimating the piety of the Irish, or by representing it as an unreal and insincere thing; nothing could be more absurd. It is thoroughly real and sincere...No other country in the world, I believe, can boast such piety as Ireland.

Filson Young: *Ireland at the Crossroads*

In no other country in the world, probably, is religion so dominant an element in the daily life of the people as in Ireland.

Sir Horace Plunkett: *Ireland in the New Century*

The March of A Nation

No man has the right to fix the boundary to the march of a nation. No man has a right to say to his country: this far shalt thou go and no further.

Charles Stewart Parnell

I go to encounter for the millionth time the reality of experience and to forge in the smithy of my soul the uncreated conscience of my race.

James Joyce: *Portrait of the Artist as a Young Man*

We have kept faith with the past, and handed a tradition to the future.

Padraic Pearse

This new Eire shall be Eire the Prosperous;
Great shall be her renown and her power;
There shall not be on the surface of the wide earth,
A country found to equal this fine country.

St. Columcille, in the sixth century.

Art and Nature Blended

But colour in an Irish setting is a thing of the moment. The poet W. B. Yeats asked: "Why do people think of eternity as a long long thing? It is the flash of light on a beetle's wing". This momentary infusion of colour is an experience which the best Irish landscape painters strove to capture, where there is a feeling that had the painter worked five minutes later the scene would have looked quite different.

Harold Clarke: *The Splendour of Ireland*

It is out of the power of the pen or pencil to do its beauties justice. I shall not venture on an attempt where my failure would be certain.

Sir Richard Hoare, writing about Killarney and its lakes in 1806.

Here, more remarkably than any place I recall, have art and nature blended their best elements in one imposing and delightful prospect. High from the road rise time-worn walls, above whose summit hangs a wealth of foliage through which flowers gleam as fresh and lovely as a maiden's eyes. Quaint buildings, many of them houses with rare histories, stand out.

Irish visitor to Youghal and Blackwater in 1910.

May The Air Bless You . . .

Every feature of the landscape, everything that we see, hear, smell and feel, enters not into the body alone, but into the soul, and helps to shape and colour it.

W. H. Hudson

May the air bless you, and water and the wind, the sea, and all the hours of the sun and moon.

J. M. Synge: *Deirdre of the Sorrows*

Still south I went and west and south again,
Through Wicklow from the morning till the night,
And far from cities, and the sights of men,
Lived with the sunshine, and the moon's delight.

I knew the stars, the flowers, and the birds,
The grey and wintry sides of many glens,
And did but half remember human words,
In converse with the mountains, moors and fens.

J. M. Synge: *Prelude*

Fields of Apple Green

The evening was calm. We struck down across the fields to the lake, crossing the terraces of bare limestone that border the eastern shore. Across the water the hills rose lavender and grey from fields of apple green.

Gibbings: *On Lough Mask*

The curlew-calling time of Irish dusk
When life becomes more splended than its husk ...

John Masefield

I have an exquiste recollection of two hours' drive at nightfall from the Cliffs of Moher to Lisdoonvarna. We drove over lonely moors gently undulating and sloping towards the shore. Presently the moon rose bathing the quiet sea in its silver light and the islets in the horizon faded away in a purple mist.

Madame de Bover: *Three Months Tour in Ireland*

The Stony Seaboard

Go to Connemara, Father, beautiful countryside, so few people.

Heinrich Böll: An Irish Diary

In the afternoon the sun came out, and I was rowed over for a visit to Kilronan. As my men were bringing round the currach to take me off a headland near the pier, they struck a sunken rock, and came ashore shipping a quantity of water. They plugged the hole with a piece of sacking torn from a bag of potatoes they were taking over for the priest, and we set off with nothing but a piece of torn canvas between us and the Atlantic.

J. M. Synge: *The Aran Islands*

Freedom Comes
From God's Right Hand

Freedom comes from God's right hand
And needs a godly train,
And righteous men must make our land
A nation once again.

Thomas Davis

They were no timorous pedants who shook and made homilies when sabres flashed and cannon roared. Our greatest soldiers sat in the Lords or Commons. Theirs was qualified preference for freedom if it were lightly won — they did not prefer "Bondage with ease to strenuous liberty".

Thomas Davis

Not in vain did (the Fenian prisoners) appeal to a chivalrous generosity — his love of constitutional liberty, his sympathy with those struggling against the severities of power.

A. M. O'Sullivan, writing of Isaac Butt's defence of Fenian suspects, 1868

The Sea Around Us

A miracle of beauty ...

William Makepeace Thackeray, writing of Clew Bay: *Irish Sketchbook*

Between Sorrento Point and Bray the lovely curve of Dublin Bay which we have just left, repeated with even lovelier effect, and the graceful cone of the Sugarloaf to the right, must remind us of Vesuvius and the Bay of Naples. In summer, the sea a translucent blue, this slice of beauty must rank with anything of its kind in the world.

Richard Hayward, writing of Killiney Bay: *Leinster*

... the harbour ... looked like a seaport scene at a theatre, gay, cheerful, neat, picturesque.

William Makepeace Thackeray: writing of Glengarrif: *Irish Sketchbook*

We stood two thousand feet above the level of the sea; Clew Bay, that magnificent sheet of water was extended at our feet, studded with countless islands.

W. H. Maxwell: *Wild Sports of the West*

Killary Bay — what use in writing about the inexpressible?

Stephen Gwynn: *Irish Books and Irish People*

Wakes

The old Bacchanalian dance may yet be found ... While the women and family weep in a corner, the men smoke and drink round the fire, joking and laughing, discussing the fairs or crops or politics or indulging in rustic buffoonery. The youth of both sexes give themselves up in dark corners to diversions that might be in place at a dance.

Mme. de Bovet: *Three Months' Tour in Ireland*

... her cousins had come
From all parts of the Kingdom
For the wake: Coffeys and Lanes from Dingle
MacCarthys and Ryans, married and single, ...

Brendan Kenneally: *Moloney Remembers the Resurrection of Kate Finucane*

Thanks to himself, my Conn will have the finest wake this day!
Wid Nancy Malone and Biddy Maddigan for keeners — There'll
be ating and dhrinking, and six of the O'Kellys to carry him out as
grand as a mimber o' parliament.

Dion Boucicault: *The Shaughraun*

The Races

A day's racing anywhere in Ireland ... will serve a variety of tastes, from those who like to look around at a pleasing scene through those who require only the hell and fun of it to those who love horses.

Kate O'Brien: *My Ireland*

National Hunt racing (or steeplechasing) began in Ireland in 1752 in Co. Cork, when one day a Mr. O'Callaghan riding Johnny Lad, a stallion, took on a Mr. Blake riding a mare called Pam Be Civil in a race from the church at Buttevant to Doneraile ... the sport that attracts the greatest number of female supporters, horse racing, also probably gains the most for Ireland in terms of international prestige

Noel Carroll: *Sport in Ireland*

It's there you'll see the jockeys and they mounted on most stately,
The pink and blue, the red and green, the emblem of our nation.
When the bell was rung for starting, the horses seemed impatient,
Though they never stood on ground, their speed was so amazing.

Galway Races (Traditional ballad)

Racing had taken place for years at Leopardstown when an Australian visitor put his stop-watch on the two-year olds running over five furlongs. "They must be the greatest horses in the world," was his verdict on discovering it took the winner a mere fifty-five seconds to cover the distance. The solution to the "greatness" was discovered when the course was measured and found to be one hundred yards short of the distance!

Michael O'Hehir: *Leopardstown Old and New*

Note: five furlongs = five-eighths of a mile.

Who Hear Thee, They Praise Thee

Oh, Danny Boy, the pipes are calling
From glen to glen and down the mountainside ....

Traditional song

It is Mary Hynes, the calm and easy woman,
Has beauty in her mind and in her face;
If a hundred clerks were gathered together
They could not write down a half of her ways.

The blind fiddler, Raftery, *c. 1840 (Translation)*

A livery I'll wear,
And I'll comb out my hair,
And in velvet so green I'll appear;
And straight I will repair
To the Curragh of Kildare
For it's there that I'll find tidings of my dear.

Traditional ballad

Who hear thee, they praise thee,
And weep as they praise,
For, Charmer, thou stealest
Thy notes from the fays!

Anonymous. Attributed to the harper Connallon — c.1670 — in
Bunting: *Ancient Music of Ireland*

Coming Home to Erin

It may be some day I'll go back to Ireland
If it's only at the closing of my day,
Just to see again the moon rise over Claddagh
And to watch the sun go down on Galway Bay.

Popular song

40

My father was now much quieter than he used to be and on the boat going over he stayed in our cabin smoking cigarettes or reading ... every once in a while though he would look up suddenly just in time to see me looking at him and whenever that happened he would jump to his feet and come over to me, pick me up and laugh and whirl me around and tell me over and over again that once we got to Ireland we would have great times together, just the two of us.

Edwin O'Connor: *All in the Family*

Island of Saints and Scholars

For once, at any rate, Ireland drew upon herself the attention of the whole world, as the great seminary of Christian and classical learning.

Kuno Meyer, writing about the early Middle Ages in *The Story of Ireland*

Christ with me,
Christ before me,
Christ behind me,
Christ in me,
Christ beneath me,
Christ above me,
Christ on my right,
Christ on my left

Breastplate of Saint Patrick

Since the coming of St. Patrick 1500 years ago, Ireland has been a Christian and a Catholic nation. All the ruthless attempts made down through the centuries to force us from this allegiance have not shaken her faith. She remains a Catholic nation.

Eamon de Valera

A Spirit to Haunt the Heart

Were all the tribute of Scotia mine,
From its midland to its borders,
I would give all for one little cell
In my beautiful Derry.

St. Columcille

The low notes she cadenced breathed very great passion. It was in the Irish she was singing. And she had a most perfect voice and her heart was single for it was about Ireland, and not about love, that she made such sweet music.

Alan Downey: *The Green Path*

Every Irish man forms some vague ideal of his country ... a spirit which has haunted the hearts and whispered a dim revelation of itself through the lips of the bards and ancient story-tellers. For this he works and makes sacrifices.

A.E. (George Russell)

Art and Artifice

In warm sunshine with hundreds lining the streets, the new austere façade of the Abbey Theatre opened its doors north of the Liffey to a distinguished crowd that came to celebrate a moment in literary history . . . a fanfare of trumpets signalled the rise of the curtain.

The Irish Press, 19 July 1966

Bravado characterised much Irish, all Anglo-Irish writing ...
There is this about us: to most of the rest of the world we are semi-
strangers, for whom existence has something of the trance-like
quality of a spectacle. Art is for us inseparable from artifice: of
that, the theatre is the home.

Elizabeth Bowen: *Pictures and Conversations*

In *Translations* Brian Friel has laid a sure and sensitive finger on
... the age-old Irish-English problem ... a complex and skillfully
made play.

Cordelie Oliver in *The Guardian*

She's A Beauty Every Line

Ah, Connemara: — you either like it or you don't. But if you do, it's like a drug. In twenty years I haven't wanted to move outside this part and if I have ventured to Galway, my heart has lifted on getting back to Oughterard, which we call the Gateway to Connemara. Yes, it's a drug to me.

The present Duchess de Stackpoole in a radio interview

Currachs, like stranded whales, lay at the head of small beaches, beaches jewelled with shells.

Robert Gibbings: *Lovely is the Lee*

When the dark flood of the ocean and the white foam rush
together
High she rides, in her pride, like a sea-gull thro' the gale;
Oh she's neat, oh she's sweet; she's a beauty every line,
The Queen of Connemara, that bounding barque of mine.

The Queen of Connemara (popular song)

The Land I Loved In ...

Where is the land I loved in?
What music did I sing
That left my ears enchanted
Inside the fairy ring?

I see my neighbours shudder,
And whisper as I pass:
"Three nights the fairies stole him,
He trod on sleeping grass."

Dora Sigerson Shorter

There is honey in the trees where her misty vales expand,
And her forest paths, in summer, by falling waters fann'd,
There is dew at high noontide there, and springs i'
                                        the yellow sand,
On the fair hills of holy Ireland.

Sir Samuel Ferguson *(Translation from the Gaelic)*

Out of such stuff as Ireland dreams are made of.

AE (George Russell)

Wild Sports and Sportsmen

Sixty years ago pounding matches were favourite amusement in the west of Ireland. It might be at some dinner before races or a fair, some fortunate owner of a great jumper would challenge a rival to the test. On the appointed day, accompanied by their friends, grooms and half the countryside, they would ride to some very difficult piece of country, and each in turn had the choice of a fence over which the other must follow or admit defeat. Large sums were often ventured on these ordeals and the most dreadrul obstacles were attempted.

Col. M. G. Moore: *An Irish Gentleman*

The toughest of them all was Tom Cosh, the famous poacher from Araglen. It was a wild class of militia man he was and the whole world knew him. He lived so close to the Araglen that he could hear the spawning fish tearing up the river outside. He'd jump out of bed and in a minute he'd have the salmon landed and back inside his cottage and he knowing that his dinner was certain for the next day.

Bill Hammond: *A Salmon Gilly Recalls*

Brian O'Malley, the head boatman whom Pat so lovingly called a *bhoy*, was the most ancient mariner I had ever shipped with, and much exceeded in appearance the seventy-three years he later confessed to; yet there was a grimness in this ordering of the course which soon inspired confidence that he still possessed more "go" than many a younger man.

Philip Green: *Days Stolen for Sport*

St. Patrick's Day in the U.S.A.

... a gala occasion with full dress parade and drill.
    Newspaper report of St. Patrick's Day, New Orleans, 1814

... these festal functions have spread all over the United States with the march of the Irish race. Every urban community gives welcome and honour to the Irish anniversary, often by impressive military and civic parades ... by eloquent pulpit utterances, by the display of flags and by great banquets attended by national, state and civic officials.
    Crimmins: *Saint Patrick's Day*

On Saint Patrick's night 1832 an Erin ball took place, the *Gazette* stating the day before that "the young sons and grandsons of Erin, young men of the first respectability give their first Ball this evening at Masonic Hall. On this occasion fashion and beauty with characteristic glow of feeling, will be exhibited in the best style. We intent to accept the invitation to attend."
    Evening Post

The commanding officer desires that the celebration of the day should not pass without having a little rum issued to the troops ... While the troops are celebrating the bravery of Saint Patrick in innocent mirth and pastime he hopes they will not forget their worthy friends in the Kingdom of Ireland ...
    from *Military Orders of the Day*,
    issued on March 16th, Morristown, New Jersey.

Plays and Players

The reception of plays here proves that not all the music halls or musical comedies that have been or will be written can extinguish the love of poetic and beautiful things which is so deeply rooted in the Irish heart

the critic Frank Fay in *Dublin,* (1900)

I have shown the Englishman to the Irishman and the Irishman to the Englishman; the Irish saint shuddering at the humour of the Irish blackguard — only to find, I regret to say, that the average critic found the blackguard very funny and the saint very impractical.

George Bernard Shaw, after the opening of *John Bull's Other Island*

The Wild Geese

The more Irish officers in the Austrian service the better. An Irish coward is an uncommon character.

Emperor Francis I, 1765

Cherish the learned Irish with a gentle heart ...

Sedulius Scotus, Irish scholar in France, to the bishop of Liège, in the late 9th century.

American Irish heroes did not leave the soft gentle Ireland celebrated in song ... they brought it with them. When their spirit burst upon this great land of the United States, they and the nation prospered.

Kevin M. Cahill : *Irish Essays*

Now let the hearts of all rejoice again
For our great earls have safely come to Spain.
— from the Tirconnell bard, Feargal Óg Mac Ward's dirge, *The Flight of the Earls*

From Glen To Glen

The village itself contains nearly a hundred whitened cottages, is romantically situated on the shore-side, in a deep ravine or sequestered glen ... in the vicinity is a little deerpark.

Glenarm, Co. Antrim, Co. Antrim, described in the *Dublin Penny Journal*, 1836

The renowned Glens of Wicklow owe their lovelinees to the varying power of resistance to weather of the rocks that form them where the upper valley lying on granite, broad and shaggy with heather, suffers a dramatically beautiful change as its river plunges over slaty schists in a cascade through limestone valleys green with pasture. There are signs on every hand of the master sculptor, ice.

Richard Hayward: *Leinster*

There are many little loughs, and in the evening what one remembers is the pure gleam of water and the dark outline of these little hills against the sky from which the water seems to have stolen the greater part of its brightness.

Sean O'Faolain: *The Great O'Neill*

On many of the small heather-bounded lakes that dot the bogs, swans may be seen in pairs, in tens, in twenties. These are the true wild swans whose bills are not orange ... but lemon-gold, the gold of Lir's coronet; and their singing is like that of many women humming.

Robert Gibbings: *Lovely is the Lee*

The Little Towns of Ireland

Do you know Bective? Like a bird in a nest, it presses close to the soft green mound of the river bank, its handful of houses no more significant by day than the sheep that dot the far fields. But at night when all its little lamps are lit, house by house, it is marked out on the hillside as clearly as the Great Bear is marked out in the sky, and on a still night it throws its shape in glitter on the water.

Mary Lavin, writing of Bective, Co. Meath: *A Likely Story*

... a serenely beautiful little spot. Silent and retired, its inhabitants few and apparently mixing little with the world.

Adare, Co. Limerick, described by the English traveller, Holmes,
in 1797

The Mall with its avenue of elms overshadowing a bright river which runs in its midst under two picturesque stone bridges is so cleanly kept as to recall a vague thought of some old Flemish town.

Mme. de Bovet writing of Westport, Co. Mayo: *Three Months'*
Tour in Ireland

The Noble Rivers

The gentle Shure that making way
By sweet Clonmell adorns rich Waterford ...

and

The goodly Barrow which doth hoard
Great heapes of salmons in his deep bosome
All which long sundred doe at last accord
To joyne in one, ere to the sea they come.

Edmund Spenser (1552-1599)

The noblest river of this country, which albeit his springe where
he riseth be but fifteen miles from his mouth yet with his many
winding crannies doth he fetch his compasse far.

The medieval chronicler Camden, *writing of the river Liffey.*

... beneath a projecting rock overhanging the lowest basin is a
grotto from which the view of the cascade is particularly
beautiful, appearing as a continued flight of three unequally
elevated foaming stages.

O'Sullivan's Cascade near Glena, *Co. Cork, Described by Wright.*

Bravely In His Charge

The Irish are strong, bold, martial, prodigal in war, haughty of heart, careless of life but greedy of glory.'

Gerald Barry, quoted in *The Irish People* by E. Hogan, S.J.

The Irish are come of as mighty a race as the world ever brought forth ... I have heard great warriors say that they never saw a more comely man than an Irishman, nor that cometh on more bravely in his charge.

Edmund Spenser: *View of the State of Ireland* (1797)

Strike the proudest tone of thy bold harp, Green Isle — the Hero is thine own.

Sir Walter Scott: *The Vision of Don Roderick*

Holy Places

Elsewhere there are places made holy by man,
But Gougane was made holy by God.

from an inscription

It is strange that Ireland's most sacred relic should have been
planted by the devil. Every Tipperary school child knows that
when the devil was flying home he took a savage bite out of the
northern hills but dropped the rocky mouthful in the centre of the
Golden Vale.

H. V. Morton, writing of Cashel, Co. Tipperary

In a quiet watered land, a land of roses,
Stands Saint Kieran's city fair,
And the warriors of Erin, in their famous generations
Slumber there.

Angus O'Gillan: *Clonmacnoise (translated by T. W. Rolleston)*

In Down three saints one grave do fill,
Brigid, Patrick and Columcille.

From the old Irish, describing the burial place of the saints in
Downpatrick, Co. Down

Horse and Hound

... a rush, a snorting announced their near approach, and a herd of deer appeared within half a stone's cast. They traversed the narrow track in single file, moving downwards. When the leading stag discovered the startled peasant, he halted, tossed his antlers wildly and neighed ... Their panic lasted but an instant; but they turned round and rushed up the hill, regained the heights and were lost in the mist.

W. H. Maxwell: *Wild Sports of the West*

Where the walls are high and rugged, double banks loom big and
wide,
Sullen bog-drains strike stark terror in your soul,
'Tis a joy to ride a hunter who can take them in his stride
When a homing hill fox plays the leading role.

Stan Lynch: *Footprints on Parchment*

To the chiefs of the Fianna it is sweeter to hear the voice of the
hounds than to seek salvation.

The legendary poet Oisín to Saint Patrick

Dear Old Dublin Town

How I love the old town, where every man is a potential idler, poet or friend.

Oliver St. John Gogarty, about Dublin

Dublin has long been celebrated as a birthplace of poets and patriots. It has been admired for the classical elegance, albeit faded, of its public edifices and residential squares. Above all, it is cherished for a way of life, humane and raffish, trivial and profound.

Richard Kain: *Dublin*

... the Dublin of old statues, this arrogant city,

Donagh MacDonagh: *Dublin Made Me*

Dublin is the nearest city to the Continent. Places here (in Paris) on a Saturday night are like Capel Street and Thomas Street. There are the same joy and excitement, as though bargaining for Sunday's dinner were a holiday.

James Joyce, in a letter to Irish poet Austin Clarke

On Market Day

Down the street comes a herd of cows. Fine horses go by with plaited manes and tails and numbered cards on their flanks. A priest stands at a corner and watches the horseflesh with his eyes; as in fact everyone does. It is all so peaceful and so drenched in sanity.

H. V. Morton: *In Search of Ireland*

At the Ould Lammas Fair in Ballycastle long ago,
I met a little colleen who set my heart aglow,
She was smiling at her daddy, buying lambs from Paddy Roe,
At the Ould Lammas Fair in Ballycastle-O!

The Ould Lammas Fair (McAuley)

Standing about were elderly farmers in swallow-tailed coats and wide black hats, younger men in caps, mackintoshes and leggings, old women in red petticoats, madonnas in shawls. Here and there an Aran Islander in his dress of speckled blue and white homespun and sandals of rough hide — "pampooties" as they call them.

Robert Gibbings, describing a fair in Galway in 1940: *Lovely Is the Lee*

74

J.F.K: One Brief Shining Moment

This is an extraordinary country. George Bernard Shaw, speaking as an Irishman, summed up an approach to life: "Other peoples," he said, "see things and say 'Why?' ... But I dream of things that never were _____ and I say: 'Why not?'"

It is that quality of the Irish, the remarkable combination of hope, confidence and imagination that is needed more than ever today ... We need men who can dream of things that never were, and ask why not ...

Like the Irish missionaries of medieval days, like the Wild Geese after the Battle of the Boyne, you are not content to sit by your fireside while others are in need of your help. Nor are you content with the recollections of the past when you face the responsibilities of the present ...

A great Irish poet once wrote: "I believe profoundly in the future of Ireland, that this is an isle of destiny, that that destiny will be glorious, and that when our hour is come we will have something to give to the world."

My friends, Ireland's hour has come. You have something to give to the world, and that is a future of peace and freedom ...

From President John F. Kennedy's historic address to the parliament of the Republic of Ireland on June 28, 1963.

Stars Like Jewels in the Gloaming

Now every sound at length is hush'd away.
These few are sacred moments. One more day
Drops in the shadowy gulf of bygone things.

William Allingham: *After Sunset*

Something in the stillness beckoned us to continue and our
passage that evening (by canal) was one of the most gentle
moments of our voyage ... The night drew on until the stars stood
like jewels in the gloaming.

Raymond Gardner: *Land of Time Enough*

There's music there
And all kinds of sweetness
In the piper's greeting
At the end of day ...

Anonymous

'Tis time at length for me to foot it homewards,
For the poets of the world lie sleeping.

Daithi Ó Bruadair, 17th century poet

The Memory of Race

An Irishman takes root in the soil of his own country. Even if he makes a home in another it has no real permanence. His dream is always to come back.

Katharine T. Hinkson: *A Union of hearts*

On Lough Neagh's bank, as the fisherman strays,
When the clear cold eve's declining
He sees the round towers of other days
In the waves beneath him shining!

Thomas Moore: *Let Erin Remember*

It was the memory of race which rose up within me . . . and I felt exalted as one who learns he is among the children of kings.

AE (George Russell)

That glorious dome that stands
By the dark rolling waters of the Boyne,
Where Aengus Oge magnificently dwells.
An early Irish poet writing about Newgrange, near Drogheda

Long Nights by the Turf Fires

They much love the sciences and liberal arts and very much
honour men of learning.

Peter Lombard in about 1600 A.D.

The history of the nation, all the *placets* of their legislators, and
all their systems — philosophical and theological — were
conveyed in the harmonious measures of sound and verse.

O'Connor's Dissertations

What is the poor Irishman's cabin? — mud! his food? – a single vegetable! Yet how quick is his intelligence, how apt his capacity; how refined his wit; how constant his attachment, how patient and untiring his industry!

George Lewis Smith, 1855

I walked the Irish hills, green in every season, and passed long nights by the turf fires to experience the world and learn how to act against it.

Henry Glassie: *All Silver and No Brass*

Where Rich and Poor Stand Equal

Whylome when Ireland flourished in fame
Of wealth and goodnesse, far above the rest
Of all that bears the British Islands name,
The gods then us'd, for pleasure and for rest,
Oft to resorte thereto, when seemed them best ...

Edmund Spenser: The Faërie Queene

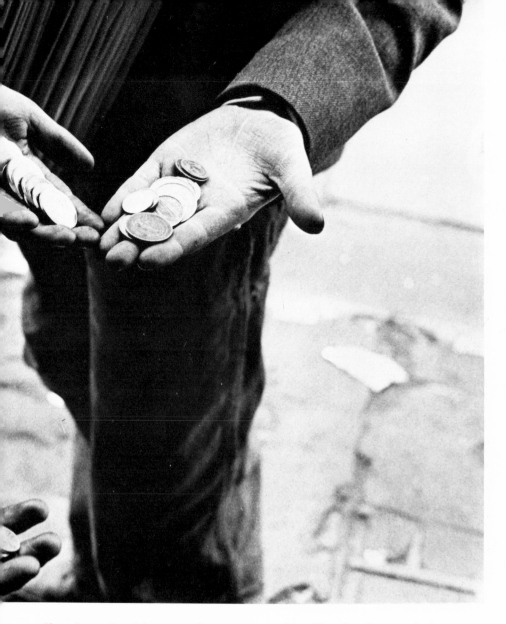

I've heard whispers of a country that lies far beyond the sea,
Where rich and poor stand equal in the light of freedom's day.

from *Wehman's Irish Song Book*

For a great man that would retire, this place would be the most
absolute, and the most interesting place in the world, both for
improvement and pleasure and healthfulness.

William Petty, writing about Kerry in 1661

The Qualities of a By-Gone Age

The garden into which we were led had the qualities of another age ... A quince tree was trained along a wall, the flame coloured blossoms contrasting delightfully with the weathered stone. Night-scented stocks and wall flowers abounded ...

Raymond Gardner, describing a garden on the river Barrow:
Land of Time Enough

The stables had kept their eighteenth century beauty. They were shaped like the buildings of an Oxford quadrangle, large enough to turn a coach and four in, and I envied the stablemen who lived there with their families, whose windows looked out on the cobbles ... I seem to remember pots of flowers on the upper windowsills but Irish countrymen seldom have flowers so perhaps it was creeper. The entrance was a long archway underneath the upper storey and could be closed with great wooden doors cut exactly to fit ... The loft above (the coachhouse) was surmounted by a clock tower, delicate and somewhat French to look at.

David Thomson, writing of Rockingham House: *Woodbrook*

A wide, beautiful valley running from east to west, sheltered between lofty and grassy hills along the crests of which are the groves and terraces of many pleasant villas.

William Bulfin, writing of Cork, 1907

On Castle Walls

The splendour falls on castle walls
And snowy summits old in story ...

Alfred Lord Tennyson, of Killarney

A crowded keep plunging like a bolt at Boyne water
It held quivering under its heart a whole province of Meath.

> Thomas Kinsella, of Trim Castle: *King John's Castle*

Kilkenny Cathedral ... full of Plantagenet knights lying in full
armour holding their swords and gazing upwards into eternity.

> H. V. Morton

The Holiest Place I Know

If I climb Hampstead Hill, than which Nature never exhibited a more glorious prospect, I confess it fine; but then I had rather be placed on the little mount before Lissoy Gate — and there take in — to me — the most pleasing horizon in Nature.

Oliver Goldsmith, *in a letter, describing his home*

Gougane Barra, a valley withdrawn, a garden enclosed, the holiest place I know.

Robert Gibbings: *Lovely is the Lee*

The women of Achill are fond of red, of which they do not mind mixing various tints; so you may see a garnet-coloured skirt with a scarlet shawl and a cherry kerchief on the head. It is picturesque to see them thus dressed going to Mass mounted two or three together on a horse.

Mme de Bovet: *Three Months' Tour in Ireland*

Cleft by the Hand of God

Looking down the drop of five or six hundred feet, the height is so great that the gannets flying close over the sea look like white butterflies, and the cloughs like flies fluttering behind them ... (you can) breathe this wonderful air which is like wine in one's teeth.

> J. M. Synge, writing of Sybil Head, Kerry

I have climbed mountains in Switzerland and in Africa, on the edge of the Sahara and Libyan deserts and I have never encountered the mystical beauty which rests in the high places of Ireland — a quality half of this world and half of the next

> H. V. Morton: *In Search of Ireland*

> A pillared chasm rude and stern
>   Cleft by the hand of God,
> From whose high arch of stone the tern
>   And seamew sweep abroad.

> Studdert Moore describing Fair head, Co. Antrim

Whether it be Slieve League in Donegal, plunging almost two thousand feet into the ocean or Mount Brandon in Kerry, westernmost outpost of Europe, or Slieve Donard, King of the Mournes — everywhere harmony and majesty of line exalt the heights ...

> M. Rivoasson: *l'Irlande*

Nonsense Galore

No, I don't know your age, *Macushla*, but whatever it is, you sure don't look it.

Spalding: *The Lilt of the Irish*

English Diner: Coffee without cream, please.
Belfast Waiter: We're out of cream, you can have it without milk.

Patrick Riddell: *The Irish – Are They Real?*

Brian O'Lynn had a house to be sure
With the stars for a roof and the bog for a flure,
A way to go out and a way to go in,
"Sure it's mighty convenient," said Brian O'Lynn.

Traditional

More Sweet Is Her Mouth

Show me a sight
That bates for delight
An ould Irish wheel wid a young Irish girl at it,
Oh no!
Nothing you'll show
Aquals her sittin' and takin' a twirl at it.

A. P. Graves: *The Irish Spinning Wheel*

Oh lovely Mary Donnelly, my joy my only best!
If fifty girls were 'round you, I'd hardly see the rest.

William Allingham

Her mind is a dove
And the wit of my love
Is more supple and swift than a bird on the wing;
More sweet is her mouth
Than wine of the south
Or all the hill honey that Greek poets sing.

George Sigerson, from the Irish

The women of Ireland are of surpassing height and exceeding beauty, and with comeliness combine matchless modesty and piety ...

Member of Papal Nuncio Rinucinni's Staff in 1645

Of Customs and Capers

Mummers go about here from Christmas till Twelfth Night. Dressed in fantastic style and singing verses suited to the occasion, they go through a whimsical dance with the aid of a piper and a "fool"! In return for their efforts to amuse, they expect a small reward at each house and in this they are seldom disappointed.

James Mooney: *Holiday Customs of Ireland*

At Downpatrick the wells were consecrated to St. Patrick, one for the eyes, others for the various limbs, and for drinking; a few mean houses by the road gave refreshment and lodging to visitors and tents were also erected; at twelve o'clock on Midsummer's Eve, the water in the wells was believed to overflow miraculously and effect cures. Invalids crowded there for a fortnight afterwards.

Máire MacNeill: *Festival of Lughnasa*

The lark is held sacred to St. Brigid because its song used to wake her to prayers every morning; if heard on her day it presages good luck ... On St. Brigid's Night in the last century (i.e. eighteenth), according to Vallancey, it was customary for every farmer's wife to bake a cake called a *barm-breac* or speckled bread. The neighbours were invited and the cake sent round with ale and pipes, and the evening was spent in mirth.

James Mooney: *Holiday Customs of Ireland*

The Noble Horse

Horses in Ireland are a drug.

> Sir William Temple, addressing the Lord Lieutenant, July
> 2nd, 1673

With the development of park courses with artificial fences,
steeplechases became far removed from the original cross-country
matches. Still the traditional concept was kept alive by various
hunts. The army also saw in this type of sport an enjoyable form of
training which developed the qualities of dash and determination
together with an eye for country.

> Col. S. J. Watson: *Between the Flags*

His manner of mounting is not unseemly though he lacks stirruppes, but more ready than with stirruppes for in his getting up his horse is still going, whereby he gaineth way.

Edmund Spenser: *View of the State of Ireland*

The end of the nineteenth century was marked by the appearance at Aintree (home of the English Grand National) of an Irish double-winner, Manifesto. In 1897 he won convincingly by twenty lengths. In the same race another Irish horse, Cathal, fell at the last fence and lay stretched out as if dead or dying but a vet discovered that he had merely swallowed his tongue; and Cathal recovered so well as to finish second the following year for the second time.

Col. S. J. Watson: *Between the Flags*

The Indomitable Irishry

Everything about Ireland, her mountains, her streams, her clouds and mist, her dew and sunshine, her music that is the expansion of them all, is made for allurement, especially for the allurement of her conquerors.

Katherine T. Hinkson: *The Adventures of Alicia*

Life springs from death; and from the graves of patriot men and women spring living nations.

Funeral oration of Patrick Pearse for
O'Donovan Rossa, 1915

O King and Maker of the world and of all that it contains, free Ireland from the perils of this strife, and knit her factions together in love.

Ua Brudair, 1689

No, I do not despair of my country. I see her in lethargy, but not in the throes of death. She is not dead, but only sleeping ...

Henry Grattan, Irish patriot

Taller Than Roman Spears

Could he (Churchill) not find in his heart the generosity to acknowledge that there is a small nation which stood alone not for one year or two, but for several hundred years, against aggression; that endured spoliations, was clubbed many times into insensibility but that each time on returning to consciousness took up the fight anew; a small nation that could never be got to accept defeat and has never surrendered her soul?

Eamon de Valera, in reply to Winston Churchill's criticism of Ireland's neutrality in World War II.

Long, long ago, beyond the misty space
    Of twice a thousand years,
In Erin old there dwelt a mighty race,
    Taller than Roman spears;
Like oaks and towers they had a giant grace,
    Were fleet as deers,
With wind and waves they made their 'biding place,
    These western shepherd seers.

Thomas D'Arcy McGee

The Joy of Spring and Summer

What a time we shall have! The long white road stretched out before us enticing us and urging us onward, the fragrance of Spring arising from the tillage, a gentle zephyr from the south laden with delightful scents.

Pádraic Ó Conaire: *Field and Fair*

The summer is coming
Over the hills;
The milk of the blackthorn
Is bursting and spills;
All day the cuckoo
In County Mayo
Breathes like a flute
As he flits high and low.

Bryan Guinness: *The Summer is Coming*

The country enjoys the freshness and mildness of Spring all year round.

Giraldus Cambrensis (c. 1147)

18th Century Players

Her manner was winning and she gained extraordinary applause. She pleased her manager, she delighted the town. In her representations of singing chambermaids roguish and fascinating, of innocent country girls wilful and witching, of widows mirthful and enticing, of viragos sharp-tongued and witty — those stock characters in the comedies of the eighteenth century she excelled — her sprightly action and merry face furnishing admirable supports to such parts. Though belonging to a profession which scandal assailed, her reputation remained untarnished and she was, as Henry Fielding expressed, "The best daughter, the best sister and the best friend" imaginable.

J. FitzGerald Molloy, writing of actress Kitty Clive: *The Romance of the Irish Stage*

During the eighteenth century no other country could boast so many notable actors — in themselves fascinating personages, they were admirably fitted by national temperament for the art in which they excelled: Peg Woffington, orange-seller and booth dancer gaining place as the first actress of her day; Spranger Barry quitting his silversmith's shop to become the idol of Smock Alley Theatre; the beautiful Miss Bellamy, daughter of an Irish peer and heroine of a hundred intrigues, arrested by bailiffs in her gilded sedan chair — all are children of the Celt ...

J. FitzGerald Molloy: *The Romance of the Irish Stage*

Garrick's powers in *Richard II* and *King Lear* were seen with delight and astonishment. When the following night he descended to the tobacco boy the public were convinced that there was nothing in human life that such a genius could not represent.

Arthur Murphy: *Life of David Garrick Esq.*

The Irish in America

Of Irish colonists in America, a large proportion everywhere stood foremost on the side of the patriots. It seemed as if providence had mysteriously used victims of Britain's cruelty — the men whom her persecution had driven from their own land — as the means of her final punishment and humiliation on foreign soil.

Dr. Samuel Smiles: History of American Independence

An Irishman, the instant he sets foot on American ground, becomes *ipso facto* an American ... East Coast Irish merchants' purses were always open and their minds devoted to the common cause. More than once Congress owed their existence to their fidelity and firmness.

Marquis de Chastellux: Travels (1786)

Daniel O'Connell's service in arousing the Irish populace was *ipso facto* also a contribution to American politics. He taught the Irish masses that while left to themselves they were powerless, yet if they threw their resources behind a political machine such as his they could exert pressure. This lesson did not recede from the minds of Irishmen when they migrated to the United States where political bossism gave the immigrant a sense of relevance in the American political structure.

Owen Dudley Edwards: American Images of Ireland

Finding Liberty Across the Sea

Eight Irishman, passionate organisers of the independence struggle, signed the Declaration of Independence. After the war an Irishman prepared the first Declaration for publication from Jefferson's rough draft. An Irishman's son first publicly read it; an Irishman first printed and published it.

A. S. Green: *Irish Nationality*

Just outside the strip of lawn that fronts Trinity College in the heart of Dublin, there stands a statue of an orator. Few Americans who see the effigy of Edmund Burke, know that it represents the same man who championed the cause of the struggling American Colonies. Irishmen have formed the vanguard in liberty's march ...

William A. Milton (1920)

(Although) he had not direct relationship with the Irish poor or those recently arrived first generation Irish but came from aristocratic family of immense wealth with deep roots in America's political life, yet (John F.) Kennedy's election showed that America was an open society, that all had a chance ...

Joseph P. O'Grady: *How the Irish became Americans*

Mother of Soldiers and Scholars

The old historic island, the mother of soldiers and scholars, whose name was heard in the roar of onset on a thousand battlefields, for whose dear love the poor homesick exile in the garret or cloister of some foreign city toiled and plotted ...

Charles Gavan Duffy

Out from many a mud-wall cabin
Eyes were searching through the night;
Many a manly chest was throbbing
For the blessed warning light;
Murmurs passed along the valley
Like the Banshee's lonely croon,
And a thousand blades were flashing
At the Rising of the Moon.

John Keegan Casey: *The Rising of the Moon.*

Sunset and Passchendaele

Just as the *belle époque* and the Edwardian interlude in England have appeared in the eyes of posterity as a golden sunset, so this period of Ireland's history has a flavour that lingers and enchants. It was the period of Ireland's great renaissance, or so it seemed — the period of the Abbey Theatre, Yeats, Joyce and intensive Celtic scholarship.

Constantine FitzGibbon: *Out of the Lion's Paw*

Dublin Castle, centre of the British administration in Ireland, was a bogus palace in a sham capital. The tea-parties and croquet upon its lawn and those of the great landowners gave pleasure and still evoke a curious nostalgia. In its ballrooms young Irish ladies danced with young officers who had not yet heard of Mons or Ypres or Passchendaele. All those who could afford it went hunting and even those who could not went racing.

Constantine FitzGibbon: *Out of the Lion's Paw*

Whole streets of men including those from the poorest parts of Belfast and Dublin marched off to die on the Somme and at Passchendaele ...　Elgy Gillespie: *Country Life Book of Ireland*

On the Banks of the Lee

Lovely, friendly, rebellious Cork ...

Bryan MacMahon: *Here's Ireland*

The spreading Lee that like an island fayre
Encloseth Corke with his divided floode.

Edmund Spenser

The bells of Shandon
That sound so grand on
The pleasant waters
Of the river Lee.

Father Prout (Francis Mahoney)

Palladian columns, gazeboes, glass-houses, teraces showed on the background misted with spring green, all stuck to the hill, all slipping past the ship ... She had never landed at Cork, so this hill and that hill beyond were as unexpected as pictures at which you say, "Oh look!" Nobody was beside her to share the moment which would have been imperfect with anybody else there.

Elizabeth Bowen: *The House in Paris*

Isle of the Blest

Irish islands are remarkably like Greek ones — the same low profile, stone walls, grey donkeys, white cabins and clear water lapping on empty beaches

Wallace Clark: *Sailing Round Ireland*

Inisfallen, in which are found woods as gloomy as ancient Druidical forests, thick with ashes and hollies, glades sunny and cheerful, bowers and thickets, without a touch from the hand of art, save the crumbling ruins.

The lake island Inisfallen, from *Murray's Handbook of Ireland* (1912)

On the ocean that hollows the rock where ye dwell,
A shadowy land has appeared as they tell,
Men thought it a region of sunshine and rest
And called it "Hy-Brasail" the isle of the blest.

Griffin: *Hy-Brasil – The Isle of the Blest*

Loveliest Village of the Plain

Dunquin, you're not a city,
But you're all the world to me!
    Felix Kearny, writing of Dunquin, Co. Antrim

Sweet Auburn! loveliest village of the plain,
Where health and plenty cheered the labouring swain,
Where smiling Spring its earliest visit paid,
And parting summer's lingering blooms delayed.
                Oliver Goldsmith: *The Deserted Village*

When he once more entered Youghal town, the pale morning
was playing upon it; nevertheless, everything was still fast asleep,
churches, shops, and houses deep in their dreams. Not a sound,
not a movement.
                Daniel Corkery: *The Emptied Sack*

The Garden of Eden has vanished, they say,
But I know the lie of it still —
Just turn to the left at the Bridge of Finea
And stop when half-way to Cootehill.
    Percy French: *Come Back, Paddy Reilly, to Ballyjamesduff*

The Sea-divided Gael

Hail to our Celtic Brethren, wherever they may be,
In the far woods of Oregon or o'er the Atlantic sea;
One in name and one in fame
Are the sea-divided Gael.

Thomas D'Arcy McGee

We drink the memory of the brave,
  The faithful and the few;
Some lie far off beyond the wave
  Some lie in Erin too;
And we will pray that from their clay
  Full many a race may start
Of true men, like you, men,
  To act as brave a part.

John Kells Ingram: *The Memory of the Dead*

Neither Hamilton nor Jefferson created in America parties that would last, but Jackson's appearance marked the emergence of the modern political boss. When the Irish arrived in the late 1840's and early 1850's they came at the right moment to participate in the perfection of the new politics as an expression of American pluralism.

Joseph P. O'Grady: *How the Irish Became Americans (1973)*

Nature Smiles

Certainly the view from the roof was worth coming up to look at. It was rough, heathery country on one side, with a string of little blue lakes running like a turquoise necklet round the base of a firry hill, and patches of pale green pasture were set amidst the rocks and heather. A silvery flash behind the undulations of the hills told where the Atlantic lay in immense plains of sunlight.

Somerville and Ross: *Experiences of an Irish R.M.*

Nature here smiles with a benevolent majesty like that of those good giants who inspire a feeling of strength tempered with calm gentleness.

Mme. de Bovet, of Giant's Causeway: *Three Months' Tour in Ireland*

Inland, the eye ranged over a space of fifty miles; and towns and villages beyond number were sprinkled over a surface covered with corn, with grass, with russet heath in beautiful alternation.

W. H. Maxwell: *Wild Sports of the West*

Below us bay sleeping sky. No sound. The sky. The bay purple by the Lion's head. Green by Drumleck. Yellowgreen towards Sutton. Fields of undersea, the lines faint brown in grass, buried cities.

James Joyce: *Ulysses*

Children at Play

When the short days of winter came, dusk fell before we had well eaten our dinners. When we met in the street the houses had grown sombre. The space of sky above us was the colour of ever-changing violet and towards it the lamps of the street lifted their feeble lanterns. The cold air stung us and we played till our bodies glowed. Our shouts echoed in the silent street.

James Joyce: *Dubliners (Araby)*

Sharon suddenly burst out laughing Maeve stared at her for a moment and then into the tankard, then she too burst out laughing. The pair of them sat there throwing back their heads, then bending forward, the sound of the one sending the other into greater fits.

Patrick Duggan: *The Golden Horseshoe*

(She) wore a scarlet bathing-cap. She made a turn, submerged, came up again not far from Dicey. — "Race you, lazy?" Thus showing how good was her mood since she lost always. For a minute more Dicey let herself lie ... Then they did race. There being no goal — no buoy, raft, rock, nothing in sight — it was racing for speed's sake.

Elizabeth Bowen: *The Little Girls*

Elegant, Eloquent Buildings

Even English lovers of Georgian architecture are a little frightened of the exuberance of Dublin — the rich and coloured traces of a southern, catholic, baroque past that England never knew.

John Harvey: *Dublin*

An elegant building, the most eloquent Dublin was to see till the coming of Gandon. Happily it can still be seen, but only with difficulty or at a distance.

Maurice Craig, of 86, St Stephens Green South: *Dublin 1660-1860*

(The cathedral's upper-storey windows) have all the exultant sensuality of the Provençal love poetry that the Mormans brought to Ireland.

Tom & Susan Cahill, of St. Canice's Cathedral, Kilkenny:
Literary Guide to Ireland

... since 1908 part of University College, this granite house has one of the most handsome fronts in Dublin, five bays wide, virile and well-proportioned with an admirable lion couchant over the door.

Maurice Craig, of 86 St Stephens Green South: *Dublin 1660-1860*

Clemency and Good Faith

There is no nation under the sun that love equal and indifferent justice better than the Irish.

Sir John Davis, Attorney General for Ireland in the reign of King James I

The Irish race possesses every charm, grace, eloquence, beauty — and misfortune.

de Lasteyrie: *Revue des deux Mondes (1854)*

The war which the Confederation of Kilkenny (the "patriot parliament") maintained was distinguished by clemency and good faith. When strong places fell into their hands they murdered no garrisons, burned no churches ... though such crimes were being committed against them at the moment.

Charles Gavan Duffy — Introduction to Thomas Davis's *The Patriot Parliament*

The Irish are the most ill treated and in all this essential qualities of heart and character, the noblest population that ever existed on earth.

Frederick Lucas (1852)

133

The Halo of a Laugh

When they see a wanderer, the old people are glad to stop and talk for an hour or more ...

J. M. Synge: *In Wicklow, West Kerry and Connemara*

We Irish when we think, and we often do this, are just as serious and sober as an Englishman; but we never hesitate to give a serious thought the benefit and halo of a laugh.

Sean O'Casey: *A Whisper About Bernard Shaw*

My generation know few happier experiences than this: to return in the height of summer to some far-away Irish-speaking district, to bathe in the local river after the long spin on cycle or in motor-car, to stroll to the nightly reunion — and shake hands with half a countryside.

Daniel Corkery: *The Rivals*

(They have) the Shakespearian art of changing the pace from serious to silly, or from rambling to crisp ...

Tom & Susan Cahill, of Irish talkers: *Literary Guide to Ireland*

The Wearing of the Green

We owe a great debt to those of our people who are scattered all over the world ... Saint Patrick brought a message of peace and brotherhood: the promotion of peace is the greatest honour we can pay to him on this day.

President Hillery's St. Patrick's Day Message, 1983

There's a dear little plant grows in our isle,
'Twas Saint Patrick himself sure that set it,
It thrives through the bog and the brake and the mireland,
He called it the dear little shamrock of Ireland.

Andrew Cherry: The Dear Little Shamrock

Situated in one of the prettiest glens in the country at about two miles from Clonmel in south Tipperary, St. Patrick's Well is arguably the most impressive spring well in Ireland, disgorging five hundred gallons of water per hour into the adjacent pool ... It has been a place of pilgrimage for generations especially on St. Patrick's Day.

Tomás Ó Duinn in The Irish Times

Irish Firsts in America

With the coming of the canal-buildings, Irish work was begun on a new church in Albany in 1839. If it was not *chic* at least it was respectable and Tallyrand and Lafayette visited it ... eventually there was a cathedral, from where Bishop John McCloskey, a gentle man who was the son of an Irish shopkeeper in Brooklyn, watched over the flock. One day he was to be made the first American cardinal.

J. Corry: *Golden Clan, the Murrays,*
McDonnells and the American Irish Aristocracy

The first public monument in this country erected to a woman was in honour of Margaret Haughery of New Orleans, an Irishwoman who devoted all her time to the alleviation of the conditions of the poor. So beloved was she that when she died the city went into mourning.

Irish Firsts in American History

In the English speaking world during the first quarter of the twentieth century the greatest playwrights were Irish — Sean O'Casey, W. B. Yeats, G. B. Shaw, J. M. Synge, and the most influential experiment was the Abbey Theatre — against this background it was logical, if not predictable, that the first serious and important playwright in the United States should have been Eugene O'Neill, an American of Irish parentage.

William V. Shannon: *The American Irish*

A Share of Heaven

That evening the harper was playing again. And his wife was there too with her fiddle. If you would hear *Teddy O'Neill* played on the harp, across the wide square in the soft evening light of the west, 'tis better for you to wear a wide-brimmed hat, for you may want to shade your eyes.

Robert Gibbings: *Lovely Is The Lee*

Soft strains of music rise
Varying through each winning measure,
Soothing every sense to pleasure.
He to whom such joy is given
Hath while here his share of heaven.

Carolan (1670-1738), translated by Thomas Furlong

His songs in general may be compared with those of Pindar: they have frequently the same flight of imagination.

Oliver Goldsmith, after hearing the blind bard, Carolan.

Dear harp of my country! In darkness I found thee,
The cold chain of silence had hung o'er thee long,
When, proudly, my own island harp, I unbound thee
And give all thy chords to light, freedom and song.

Thomas Moore

Beauty to Take Your Breath Away

Oh, but our Irish woods are lovely today!
The trees are young knights, in whose helms the proud
plumes quiver;
Singing lustily goeth the wind on his way;
The voice of a naiad chants in the reeds by the river.

Katherine Tynan Hinkson: *In the May*

We were rewarded by one of those views that take your breath away with their beauty. I long to know more of the ancient Gaelic names of these hills ... Here of old the ger-falcon and savage wolf bred, and the red deer roamed; here the wild arbutus blooms in profusion ...

Evelyn Hardy: *Summer in Another World*

143

Keepers of the Christian Flame

The Irish hermit Muircheartach settled in Regensburg in the middle of the eleventh century. Joined by Irish pilgrims, he and the Irish community had the church of Weihsankt Peter presented to them, and they later built a larger monastery and church of St. James. This became the mother house of a dozen Irish Benedictine foundations in Germany and Austria known as Schottenkloester.

Tomás Ó Fiaich (Cardinal Primate of All Ireland): *Irish Cultural Influence in Europe*

The history of Ireland in the Middle Ages is something astonishing and at the same time admirable. The ancient world had collapsed, Rome and her empire were no more than ghosts and nostalgic pictures. All over the West, unchained violence had substituted for imperial order a chaos of darkness. It was then that from a distant island, men set out for the Christian conquest of the continent.

Henri Daniel-Rops: *The Miracle of Ireland*

The Irish monastery at Glastonbury, was founded in a district colonised from Ireland and later claiming to possess the tomb of St Patrick. Irish pilgrims often visited it and were received at the court of Alfred the Great.

Tomás Ó'Fiaich (Cardinal Primate of All Ireland): *Irish Cultural Influence in Europe*

Genius in Abundance

Genius the Irish have certainly had in abundance. Their imaginative energy seems inexhaustible. It finds expression in their love for poetry and legend, in their cultivation of eccentricity and their delight in personality.

Richard Kain: *Dublin*

The people of Ireland are warm and friendly, calm and unhurried, dry in their wit and strong individualists.

Europe With Pictures: (Sterling Publishing Co., New York)

Ireland is a small country where the greatest questions of politics, morality and humanity are fought out.

Gustave de Beaumont: *l'Irlande Politique*

Ireland is a country in which the political conflicts are at least genuine: they are about something. They are about patriotism, about religion, or about money: the three great realities.

G. K. Chesterton: *George Bernard Shaw*

The Heart of Ireland

She sang of the black rose. And the dark bloom was a sorrowful way of picturing Ireland, the most beautiful flower in the garden of the world with the shadow of woe colouring its silken petals.

Alan Downey: *The Green Path*

Melodious Erin, warm of heart
Entreats you; stay not then apart

William Allingham: *Songs and Poems*

Ireland is many kinds of country and adaptable to many uses. First of all, let us not forget, the land exists as the home and centre of its own race . . . Whatever else she is, she is a natural God-given playground. Come to think of it, we have an island lulled all around in a continuity of peace, of golden silence and innocence that truly cannot in such sustained immaculacy be found elsewhere now in Europe, save in the Aegean Sea.

Kate O'Brien: *My Ireland*

Blarney Galore

You haven't met Saint Gobnait? Oh, but you must meet her.
She's lovely! You'd love her! She blinds your enemies for you.
Sure, every time the inspector comes into the office I whisper to
St. Gobnait and he never sees a wrong entry.

A tale from Co. Cork

"What would you do, Jer, if you won a million?"

'Begor, I suppose I am too old to go round the world ... Yerra,
I'm not. 'Tis round the world I'd go."

A 79-years old Corkman

As beautiful Kitty one morning was tripping
With a pitcher of milk from the fair of Coleraine,
When she saw me she stumbled, the pitcher down tumbled,
And all the sweet butter-milk watered the plain.
"Oh what shall I do now? 'Twas looking at you now,
Sure, sure, such a pitcher I'll ne'er meet again!
'Twas the pride of my dairy! Oh Barney Mac Cleary
You're sent as a plague to the girls of Coleraine!

An Irish Ballad

May the saints be surprised at your success!

West Cork wish.

'I Wish I Could Borrow Your Face"

My way of joking is to tell the truth. It's the funniest joke in the world.

George Bernard Shaw: *John Bull's Other Island*

The long and remarkable line of Irishmen who write successfully for the English stage owes a great debt to the vigour and raciness of speech in Ireland. Irish modes may be detected again and again in the speeches which Goldsmith writes for his characters. "I wish I could borrow your face," says the imposter in *The Vicar of Wakefield* — a typical Irish sally. "I am my own man again," says Tony Lumbkin when he escapes marriage.

A. de Blacam: *A First Book of Irish Literature*

Seer, saint and sage, it is on the stage that Shaw's effective influence did most work, work in a great way, for God (should God exist), work for man, and work for the Theatre . . . (He knew that) by laughter you can destroy evil without malice.

Sean O'Casey: *A Whisper About Bernard Shaw*

Through Streets Broad and Narrow

... well-built, airy, stately streets ...

William Makepeace Thackeray, of Dublin

... environment produces the qualities we associate with Dublin ... nowhere better seen than in connection with Dublin freedom of mind and wit. Even immigrants of middle age acquire the Dublin spirit ...

John Harvey: *Dublin*

In Dublin's fair city, where the girls are so pretty,
I first set my eyes on sweet Molly Malone,
As she wheeled her wheel-barrow
Through streets broad and narrow,
Crying cockles and mussels, alive-alive O!

She died of a fever, for no-one could save her
And that was the end of sweet Molly Malone,
But her ghost wheels her barrow
Through streets broad and narrow,
Crying, 'Cockles and mussels, alive-alive-O!

Traditional Dublin Song

The World's End

This island is the world's end. Beyond the wide Atlantic drives its thunderous tides backwards and forwards beating on the land time out of mind, a hammer on the heart, and the storms of the west race from the huge infinity of sea, gathering anger and split their bellies and their fist of rage against the island's shattered, silent mountain.

Sean Jennet, writing of the Great Blasket Island, in *The Cloth of Flesh*

The old historic island, the mother of soldiers and scholars, whose name was heard in the roar of onset on a thousand battle-fields, for whose dear love the poor homesick exile in the garret or cloister of some foreign city foiled and plotted ...

Charles Gavan Duffy, Irish patriot, quoted in *A History of Modern Ireland* by Edward Norman

The Photographs

The Sources

When a teacher suggested photography as a career I laughed. The humour was not shared, however by my mother: to her the notion conjured up images of selling picture souvenirs to tourists on Dublin's O'Connell Bridge.

Maternal instincts may have been right after all, because now I spend most of my time out on the streets. Like others of this school I watch and wait for those magic moments when the light or the expression is right. The apparatus is simple, the approach direct. There are no lights or make-up. The aim is to observe, unobserved. The art is in seeing, the rest is familiarity with technique and, as such, no more important than the ink in the pen of the storyteller.

A few years ago a group of like-minded photographers came together, and from their combined print collections a library was started called **Source.**

At first, apart from myself, there were people like Fergus Bourke, Tod Tuarch and John Gilbert, and soon others, like Robert Ashby, joined. The print collection grew larger, and within a year of two it had become international with strong connections in Britain and America.

One thing led to another, and ambitions probably exceeded themselves when a gallery for public exhibition was opened in the drafty semi-dereliction of a basement in Henrietta Street in downtown Dublin. Photographic images produced by the famous and the celebrated shared wall space and monthly shows with a passing parade of emerging talents.

That gallery is now gone, but the collection continues to grow. Whether it is the largest or the most diverse set of Irish prints is for other people to argue about, for the emphasis always was and remains that of illumination rather than illustration.

The same whimsical trickery that gives yeast to the scribe and mystery to the poet is part of the atmosphere here. It is no mistake to call a cobweb an "Irish chandelier," for, who knows—it may have been, or is, if you know the right way to look at it. Even stones laugh, and only last century the brothers O'Shea were dismissed because their carvings, three stories up, poked fun at their employers! There is nothing new in this, Giraldus Cambrensis, visiting Ireland seven hundred years ago, saw the beautifully decorated gospels, and he could well have believed the tale of an angel appearing as guide and inspiration.

Like the musician or the storyteller, we still talk about "the gift," and look on "ability" as the poor relation. Now look on the work of people like Bourke, Doyle, Tuach, Ashby and others, and see that there never was a question about ability. The more appropriate word is "gift." That should come as no surprise, for how could the most recent of the media, hardly out of the cradle at little over a century, fail to respond so readily to forces already ancient?

TOM KENNEDY
The Source Collection
LEIXLIP,
CO. KILDARE,
IRELAND.